ALL
its
CHARMS

ALL

its

CHARMS

For Elle —
* Who knows the stories — and*
charms — of this beautiful
island and its people. So glad to
be here with you!

POEMS BY

KEETJE KUIPERS

AMERICAN POETS CONTINUUM SERIES, No. 171

BOA EDITIONS, LTD. ✳ ROCHESTER, NY ✳ 2019

First Edition
19 20 21 22 7 6 5 4 3 2 1

For information about permission to reuse any material from this book, please contact
The Permissions Company at www.permissionscompany.com or e-mail permdude@
gmail.com.

Publications by BOA Editions, Ltd.—a not-for-profit corporation
under section 501 (c) (3) of the United States Internal Revenue
Code—are made possible with funds from a variety of sources,
including public funds from the Literature Program of the National
Endowment for the Arts; the New York State Council on the Arts,
a state agency; and the County of Monroe, NY. Private funding
sources include the Max and Marian Farash Charitable Founda-
tion; the Mary S. Mulligan Charitable Trust; the Rochester Area
Community Foundation; the Ames-Amzalak Memorial Trust in
memory of Henry Ames, Semon Amzalak, and Dan Amzalak; and
contributions from many individuals nationwide. See Colophon on page 76 for special
individual acknowledgments.

Cover Design: Sandy Knight
Cover Art: "Calla Lily 'Sunshine'" by William Rugen
Interior Design and Composition: Richard Foerster
BOA Logo: Mirko

Library of Congress Cataloging-in-Publication Data

Names: Kuipers, Keetje, author.
Title: All its charms / poems by Keetje Kuipers.
Description: First edition. | Rochester, NY : BOA Editions, Ltd., [2019] |
    Series: American poets continuum series ; no. 171 | Includes
    bibliographical references.
Identifiers: LCCN 2018050057 (print) | LCCN 2018055221 (ebook) | ISBN
    9781942683773 (ebook) | ISBN 9781942683766 (paperback :alk. paper)
Subjects: LCSH: American poetry—21st century.
Classification: LCC PS3611.U4 (ebook) | LCC PS3611.U4 A6 2019 (print) | DDC
    811/.6—dc23
LC record available at https://lccn.loc.gov/2018050057

BOA Editions, Ltd.
250 North Goodman Street, Suite 306
Rochester, NY 14607
www.boaeditions.org
A. Poulin, Jr., Founder (1938–1996)

For Nela

And for my mother

Contents

※

Becoming

The streets were glass, the cars and salt-bellied
trucks slid across them—perfect pirouettes

just past the light's red. Beyond my frosted
windshield were the animals, and beyond

the animals: silence, baled hay like spools
of thread scattered by a careless hand. In

the next season would I become just one
more hillside of purple vetch, unwanted

too-muchness sprung from a gravel pit's mouth,
dead butterflies in my teeth? There were ten

thousand ditches where I could have lain my
body down. When I saw that early spring

meadowlark—one-winged, flapping in the road—
I pressed my heel to its chest, to the earth.

Landscape with Sage and the Names of My Children

I picked all the flowers, I palmed all the stones.

I dropped the nameless insects onto my tongue
and felt their black wings unfurl. I held the dead

buck by his antlers and dragged him through the sage,

brought my teeth to the tender bridge of ribs and fed
until the glossy maggots overtook me.

I climbed the red rocks robed in their red dust.

I put the earth—all its charms—within me,
into each waiting pocket. Lip and ear.

What will happen when my body can no longer

hold this fragrant salt, its hardened tears,
inside? Let mine into the dirt. The names

I've chosen for my children are already fast

across the sky like the ochre feathers that frame
the blackbird's shrug. There is no such thing

as a scar, no matter how much I want

to be one. Every birth—even the wings
of the caddis lifting from the river

in a shroud—a momentary hunger.

The elk my father shot

is an imagined butterfly of flesh—
thin cannon bones pinning back its winged hide

like a boxed *anartia amathea*
amathea, all white speckled gristle

and silver tendon seam—when he calls me
from the mountaintop and leaves his breathless

message (afraid, at last, of what he's done)
telling of the bow, the arrow, his tin

pan trembling heart and shaking arm, quiet
so as not to scare away the grazing

ghost he's made, as if this yearly taking
of a life were a talisman carried

in his pocket beside the knife, a charm
against entropy, his own brittle bones.

The House on Fish Hatchery Road

When I see the neighbor's kids playing kick-the-can, I know
it isn't a can. Instead, some slim gift of faulty flesh

floats at the tips of their sneakers—squirrel? robin? I go

inside and stick the needle in my soft-soft belly,
count to ten as I push the plunger down. Outside

the bathroom window, the dog runs from leaf pile to leaf pile,
pissing his delight.
                    And on the neighbor's picnic table
a green beer bottle sits in the sun, fat with unfinished

cigarettes. Someone's peeled the label off all the way
around and left it there, wanting and half-full of nothing.

Unmade child, I dream you despite everything—the beakers

filled with blood, the sudden taste of metal—whatever
we're meant for when it comes for us ready or not.

Ars Poetica Composed in Exile

I've lost track of those seasons: snow

on the hilltop, while along the tracks
that laced the river's fattened sleeve,

yellow trees—were they feathering

into bloom or withering their leaves?
In the sleet and thaw, the cranes

returned in pairs of prehistoric song,

and each barn stood a redheaded flame
against the frozen page, path of ice

like ash beneath the dripping eaves. Words

might come up like fireweed on a hill twice
burned or like morels burr-buried

in the damp hips of cottonwoods.

So why can't I find the ones to marry
myself to that place again?

Like a pronghorn calf stumbling across

the frosted creek that's drowned ten men—
something finally to make me light on

these words of return: culvert, corn snow, home.

Native Species

In the spring the men come out again to clear the land,
      yellow Cat dozers popping up on distant hillsides

like morels to be collected after the first warm days
      of May. In fields studded with the rhinestone glitter

of purple knapweed, machines nose aside whatever lingers
      too long in the path: stones laid down by a glacier's

swollen body, a rain-washed pair of child's underwear,
      white-spangled fawn fresh from the belly of before-this-world.

Untouched? No such thing. Razed, plowed under, laid
      to rest only to have soil peel back from the jaw bone.

What hasn't been populated by trespassers, remade from
      the inside out? No wonder my body is finally doing the dirty

work it's always wanted to, spiraling deep within itself to make
      from this wildness something that doesn't care if it belongs.

First Trimester

Pulling plump ticks off the dog, imagining
how the late-day rain must make the ink

caps grow, even counting fireflies who rise
from my lawn like the reluctant sparks

of a resurrected campfire—every act
is an act of waiting. But when I go

inside to turn the fan on my damp body
or stand dizzy at the kitchen sink

to fill a glass, I have no flickering
yet to conceive of. It's in my room's dim

mirror I find the girl, my mother, every
thing I'm afraid of not becoming.

At the Arlee Pow-Wow with My Unborn Child

Past the pup tents and teepees, just beyond

Mo's Indian Fry Bread Tacos, children
are doing the Snake Dance. On the highway,

two semis pass, each slung with half a house,

and deer, leading their speckled young
through dead grass, give a shiver. Little swimmer

of shallow waters, diver of lights-out

interior oceans—who am I to teach you
how to dance? I buy earrings made from porcupine

quills, lemonade from the most expensive

stand, the one where white boys from town
crush thick huckleberries into the ice,

and I'm embarrassed for myself again.

On Needing to See a River

The tea-stained mug, my mother's
voice on the phone saying *contraction,*

this almost-animal working its paper
ankles and pinkening birch-bark heels

inside me. There is some need
for a river among this, some swelling

to match my own, some sunken, rounded
stones to ground this shimmering surface.

At the Museum of Trades and Traditions

Here is the tool with the delicate
handle designed to turn a tree trunk

into a pipe for channeling water. And here
is the tortoise shell carved into combs

of paisley gold. Here are the tin stamps
once pressed into warm butter to raise

the outline of a milkmaid or sunrise
on its hardening surface. Here the tobacco horns,

here the looms, here the little knives
and the elegant silver-plated pistols. We say,

Which job would you have picked?
Butter churner or glassblower? Blacksmith

or weaver? Though, as women, we wouldn't
have had so many options. Unlike my daughter,

whose father I chose from a list of hair
and eye color, narrowing the field by height

and weight and college major. Someday I'll find
that tool in a museum, the squat centrifuge,

the gasping seal of its lid, the gentle click
and whir as it swirled the sperm into a thin serum.

Or perhaps the slight catheter designed
to angle past the cervix and into the ether

of my womb. There, on velvet, under a soft light
in some airless case, the tools that made me a mother.

Georgia

Last week you told me I need to decide
if I'm in love with you. Now, red clover

spattered in the ditches, I watch everything
give itself up to the light as I cross

the state line on my way to answer you:
dogwood trees and effusive azaleas,

even the dead armadillos, belly
up to the sun. I still don't know what holds

me back. The sign on the car I pass says
Gone for gas, but that's a lie. Kudzu wound

through the tires, leaves pressed to the glass
where anyone can see the dust on the dash.

Still Life with Nursing Bra

Fall open, unfold me. Hook and eye
undone with one hand, fingers that know
their way now in the dark. You contain
me: underwire circling my breasts in
half-bangle like the copper bracelets
lemniscating wrists of women who've
never worn bras, never held back
their multitudes. You of the hidden
crab-apple bruise yellowing on my
chest. You of her ecstasy, eyes rolled
back in her head, hands in her sweat-
damp hair. You: milk that rivers down my
skin, shimmering of hunger, the want
of a wet mouth. Nursing bra—black, nude,
electric orange and lace-trimmed, tucked in
the back of the drawer or hung dangling
from a doorknob—I once fumbled
with you, stale of the dentist's lobby
cut by a thin mewling that made us all
shiver, the waiting room's terrified
ripple as I struggled with the clasp
that kept me from spilling open. Instead,
the leaking through, a sticky flower
blooming down my chest, until I wrenched
you free, flapping and fearless, one
wing taking flight from my breast.

Outside the New Body

One day I woke up   in a new body
one that contained another   and it made
      me dizzy   Now you pull   your hand from your
mouth   as if to show me something   I've known

never

      Like those birds   carrying mouthfuls
of steam   all the stark winter months   I held
you in my body   long as I could   Weighted
then with sadness   too   my fear

      you

might dissipate a fever   brief and
      untethered as the man I saw   dancing
wrapped   in a bearskin rug   head passing through
its teeth, its tender jaws   I had never held

anyone so close

      your eyes inside my
eyes   tongue inside my tongue   Now when I cup
your sleeping face   against the bow of my
shoulder   arrow notched   I am just waiting

one more moment

      before I let you go
I know   the quiver   of your heart is out-
      side the inside of me   What to do with
this new   body you left behind   the light

that streams through   its too-thin walls of fraying silk?

Getting the Baby to Sleep

Sometimes the baby can't reconcile
the self with the self—too hungry
to eat, too tired to sleep. I know

the feeling. Oh, America, on those nights
when you are too beautiful for me
to continue to forgive you any longer—

for allowing us to kill each other
with your graceless bullets or exile our
neighbors across the fences of your fictitious

border or argue over the ownership
of each young girl's body as if its freedom
is a lie she must stop telling herself—

I go out into your radiant arms.
The baby and I drive through your streets,
over the bridge and its light-chipped

waters, under a moon so big, so full
of itself that though I know it belongs
to the world, it can't be anything but

American. I hang my arm out the window
and skim the air like touching skin.
I breathe you in, and the baby sleeps.

Migration Instinct

Today the wife of the last man who made me lonely
is having a baby. Oh, October: we all want

to get up and leave, crawl out of our flesh sacks and fly.
Back when I was someone else this would have been a day

for wallowing, for bumming a cigarette off some
hot, filthy man and downing gin at noon. I'd have basted

my eyelids with green shadow, tossed less-than-delicate
looks across the room at strangers still full of all

the sweet possibility I could muster. It would
have been a tear-down-the-street-blowing-stop-signs day,

a salmon-omelet-on-the-maxed-out-Visa afternoon—
anything to drive off the low growl of nostalgia.

But I've got dishes to wash, tiny sock after sock
to fold. Sadness is so much work. Angry takes too much

time. And there's my own daughter, mouth to my breast
as she winks in the lamplight, sucking it all right out of me.

Landscape Without

In the neighbor's backyard, a woman cuts
her husband's hair, circling him in the chair

with her clippers, a bee readjusting
its approach. It's a day so mild no one

cares about anything: the daffodils
slutting themselves at the base of a tree,

the fat dogs doing their best impressions
of the dead. I sit in my car, phone in

my hand, and wonder what makes it so hard
for one person to understand another

while my neighbor gently buzzes the fine
hairs around the ruddy petal of her

husband's left ear. I look around the yard
and ask myself which metaphor I am—

The winter-downed telephone line? The tree
pimpled with tiny unopened buds? Not

one of them can make it possible
for me to say the thing between us now.

Still Life with Small Objects of Perfect Choking Size

Nothing so obvious as a gumball,
a coin. Instead, the cap

to the chapstick, or, somehow,
the moon: Lips parted, tongue

still, the tiny blackness
of her mouth's small pit

just large enough to slip
that lunar white marble inside—

blind cat's eye, milky stone.
Why does she want to take

herself from me? Somewhere
in the past I'm a girl

doing a cartwheel for the last time—
feet in the air, spin of a body

propelling itself upside down,
the whole world turning while

I turn. No one knows
it's the last time, not even I do.

Don't be so eager, I want to say
to us. In the August singularity,

the world tilts on its axis,
and our days slide into darkness—

one thing beginning, another ending,
everything undone from within.

At the Small Town Drag Show

Watching Daisy Pukes take the dollar bill
between her teeth, shake her fake tits in each

boy's peach-fuzz face, I recall my once-praised
body as it comes alive again: long

forgotten cat now raised from its shallow
backyard grave. Cat with sweat on its fur, cat

that nightly screamed below the kitchen's glass,
cat whose backbend stretch of joy raised her pink

pinhole to the sky. Daisy's high-heel boots
scuff the floorboards, her nylon blend lashes

flutter under fluorescents, and I feel
a tingle somewhere—my knees? my tongue?—

as I pour my sex, its proud performance,
back into this dress I've worn like a shroud.

Springtime Makes Us Want

The old woman who walks my street
each afternoon, head bent to the book

in her hands, wants to not be hit
by a car. The oil slicking Galveston Bay

wants to dress the feathers
of migrating birds in purple-black

sheen—make them all into crows,
dead crows. And don't I want things, too?

My daughter to press her mouth
to my breast and release me from

my own swelling sweetness. When
I drive my car down the pollen-sprayed

streets, every branch gushing
at the tips, I won't think about

what rumbles in the engine, why
I'm so glad to burn it all up.

Love Note

Does any of us remember   the first
moment of touch   Bird fallen from
feeder into the cat's parted paws   leaves
flabbergasting   the pool's unsettled
surface   This poem is a double-yolked
egg   concealed   in the unlit depths
of the fridge   it is a note
that says   I don't know how to love
But the same rain that makes the guttered
garbage float   is dripping
from the ends of your unexceptional
hair   And here I am again   examining
my wet hands   spilled poppies
where everything suddenly gathers   I won't
apologize for love   the way it looks when I
wear it   cheap   ill-fitting   and loose
at the throat   a towel a child has tied into a cape

Landscape with Ocean and Nearly Dead Dog

Should I lay him on the slab at the vet's? Let
somebody else do the work? Or back at home

in the yard, my coward's hand on the syringe,
the last of the bird song in our ears? Now I find

one pink shell, one gray, watch my daughter
knee-deep in waves as a child swims toward her

chewing flecks of styrofoam. *It's chicken,* says the girl,
Eat it. And the ibis eyeing them, god-only-knows

in its gullet. What makes me want to take these fractures
home? The shale of blue plastic covered in stony

warts, starfish arm severed in the night, feelers
still tickling the air. I'll hold the dog's head

in my lap, let him smell on my salted hands
every little thing we're willing to give up.

My Brother Says My Milk Smells Different

Meaning different from his wife's, meaning
a melody all my own, playing in my body
like the song the headphoned girl on the bus
mouths the words to—silent for the rest of us, a tune
only when we press her lips to our ear.

A friend stored her milk in a humming freezer,
rows and rows of pumped bottles, icy blue-white
diamonds tucked away in the basement, glowing
dumbly each time she pulled open the door—
plenitude, mass, sweetness contained.

Or unleashed: two long seams of milk, petalled
stains flushing my shirt front, the way migrating
monarchs hang in delicate clumps from eucalyptus—
near-still garlands, just the faint backbeat
of their wings ready to erupt into song.

At Golden Gate Park with You

To watch the sea change
                        color as steam-
liners move across
                        it. To watch your eyes

change color as my
                        hands move across you.
There is no perfect
                        metaphor for the act

of turning you on.
                        But I try anyway,
until the slick-skulled
                        koi, the nasturtiums

sweating on the vine—
                        everything
becomes your body
                        twisting in my arms.

Shooting Clay Pigeons After the Wedding

Up the snow-slicked hill, the truck's tracks behind
us like the drag of our twin wedding trains,

until through the something-blue windowpane
the valley floor opened, clear as my mind

just after I'd lifted your veil's tulle blind.
The shotgun's recoil shivered its dull pain,

and yet what pleasure taking my sure aim
as disk after gold clay disk flew and whined.

I held my breath and the gun like a man,
shattering the altar of cloud-laced sky.

I was doing it by instinct—that new
muscle near my heart. I wanted more than

anything to be a natural. I
wanted more than anything to be true.

Donetsk

The tragedy on today's radio sounds like my daughter
trying to say "donuts" for the first time,

or like the chirp of the two lovebirds I loved for just
a year when I was fourteen, their eager

hiccup when I took them from their cage
and placed one on each shoulder. It could be

the voice of the waitress at Cracker Barrel,
a pen in the corner of her sour pucker,

asking if I've finished with my plate of soggy
pancakes, or the pop and crack of my old

neighbor's knuckles as he grasps the axe
and takes a swing. Or maybe it's the hushed

suck when I pull the plug from the tub drain
after the baby's shat in her bathwater

and I have to wash it out and start all over again.
It sounds far away, the way everything does

here where it's always warm, always unseasonably
sunny, where I'm always somebody's mother

turning the pages of some forgettable picture book
on the other side of the distant world.

Yardwork

Every weekend I give you chores:
rake, fill feeders, give the grass a mow.
My body, too, is told to work, while yours—

lush and flowering on all scores—
is asked to wait for what mine might grow.
All week long I do my brand of chores,

priming the flesh's barren moors
with needled prescriptions designed to sow
these unnamed seeds that are not yours.

Making love some evening might restore
us to our freer former selves, though
touching could be one more chore

of prodding hands I've learned to ignore.
Now the nurses peck my limbs like crows,
discouraging my body's urge for yours—

I resist planting and can't bear play. But more
than plotted cycles, this I know:
Some things can't be fixed through faithful chores,
my body failing to work apart from yours.

Glassblower's Glossary of Flaws and Defects

Small parison, slack and heavy bauble,
I breathed you into being with my want,

my belief in your fragile form I'd thought
to coax to life with pinpricks and prayers.

From my belly's furnace, I imagined
pulling you whole—beveled, and thinly

gilded with meconium's sharp-scented glaze.
Within my body's medicated light,

your molten form grew rivets and grooves, frit
coloring and clinging to your lucent bones,

lengths along which you might someday be touched.
When you refused conjuring, I carried

for months a dullness in my mouth, still not
knowing I had burnt my tongue on desire.

Self-Care at the Playground

The sidewalk grows a golden fur

of fallen leaves, and on the swings
in the park, a woman sounds

an off-key minor chord, her body

participating in a kind of joy
uncomfortable for the rest of us.

In my pocket, the small screen

waits for me, each page queued
to show me everything I make myself

know, including a man in his car,

his girlfriend in the passenger seat,
the child in the back. Later, I will watch

the bullets empty his body again and again.

I am not important, I repeat
to myself as I pump my legs,

looking up to watch through the sky—

itself a glowing screen—twenty-seven
undulating shades of white—the colors

of crushed and strewn shells—

as the leaves fall through it
with their messages of red.

Outside the Refugium

*The myths and folklore of traditional people the world over are replete
with descriptions . . . of refugia, the inviolable strongholds of animals
and plants . . . missing only the human, and holding out the promise
of a less tumultuous future.*

—Barry Lopez, *Home Ground: A Guide to the
American Landscape*

The sparrow is an opened book, an angel

parted down the breast, head turned to the side
so one black eye can search the stippled sky

in ecstasy as the magpie straddles and works

the body over with famished care. I sit
beneath the silver olive and watch, rub

a single fruit between my thumb and forefinger

until it slips its furred skin, until the dark pit
rolls there. No pool of blood, just her shit-stuck feathers

and a cloud of aspen leaves painted with drought's

dusty watercolor scar. When he finds the heart,
the magpie tucks it down his throat, a jewel

hidden in haste before the border's crossing.

Yes, the world has always been this fragile,
he says as he lifts her by the ribcage

and carries her off to where I cannot see.

Picking Huckleberries as the World Ends

Our family ranged across the tinder-dry hillside,
baby safe for now within some beetle-pocked

ponderosa's shadow, knapweed flocking her cheeks,
the fires all around us, everything burning as we

move from bush to bush, soft-filtered shadows of birds
crossing our backs, a dusting of ash on the still leaves,

and the berries we pluck tart, parched, smaller
than ever and tarnished by heat. It's not the end,

love, though when it comes, I hope we'll shelter in
the consolation of touch, that human habit you and I

have fallen out of. If there's another way to live
on this earth, let us be brave and find it together.

Landscape with Child

The bats come on at dusk, playing between
the pine trunks, shadow puppets cast against

the lake's silvering surface. I hold you: harp
and harpist, bodies bound. All day power-

lines above our heads sizzled in the heat,
a million insects sifting to the ground

in a shower of fine wings. Your absence
is impossible, unimaginable.

You can't ever be gone from me—a prayer
I hold under my tongue like a dark pill

I'm afraid to swallow. Not like my friend's
baby, not like the child lost in the river's

teeth. Where is the bear I promised you
we'd see? We must look again tomorrow.

On the Haunted Hayride with Audrey

Who, by the way, is dead. Who hanged herself
in the neighbor's woods last week, just in time

for Halloween. Whose lank green hair I know
only from the *Missing* signs posted

on telephone poles, now rain-logged and peeling
in ragged strips of zombie bandages.

Who should be here tonight not as a ghost
but as a teenager, like these other ten

dressed in scarecrow rags, who blank-faced
writhe to the latest pop hit, spooking

my own small daughter. *It's alright,* I tell her,
towhead hidden in hay bales. *Just teenagers.*

Audrey, I don't have to be your mother
to be furious with you. When a specter

zip-lines across the field, gown aglow
with battery-operated ectoplasm,

my child lifts her eyes and gasps, *They forgot
the angel wings, Mommy,* so that I want

to stand up and yell, *Audrey, get down from there
this minute!* Stop scaring me half to death.

Laying On of Hands

As when standing too close
to the violinist, one hears above
the music of horsehair and catgut
the musician's labored breathing
as he sweats to press his notes upon
the air with increasing urgency,

so the priest stepped too close to me,
and laying his hands on my already
too-permeable belly straining
at the weave of skin's fragile cloth,
intoned above your heart's
beating—which I could not

know or feel but remained
certain of every hour
of every day nonetheless—
a blessing of his own making,
which I'm sure he believed
to be both music and comfort

but which I heard as curious
reverse osmosis curse, one meant
to mark your soul as surely as if
he'd applied the delicate
speckle of mole I found
on your left ankle the day

you were born—signet tipped
into hot wax—so that I held
my breath and so hoped to hold
yours, counting the seconds inside
of which I could by some mother's
magic keep you safe one moment longer.

I buy my white daughter a black doll

and she cries and she sleeps and she rides
through our kitchen in a pink stroller. She takes
a tiny bottle in her pursed lips, and every night

she takes a bubble bath. As my daughter drapes
a washcloth across her brown shoulders
and down the delicately curved back, I think

about the man I loved years ago—his elbows,
his knees, those ashy places I caressed without
understanding—and how his mother told me

make sure he moisturize, as if she agreed I had
any business caretaking his body in a country
that would rather see him dead. What do I

think I can teach my daughter, especially when
I've still learned so little? Only that we might all
be transformed by our own unknowing love.

The Great Lakes

My wife, the one I thought I'd never have—
because does any of us believe we deserve
to be happy in this life?—lets my daughter paint
her toenails a sloppy silver as my aunt smokes
a second cigarette and pages through photos
on her phone so I can see how the car looked
after my cousin wrecked it last month
in a past-midnight field near the poultry
processing plant just a half mile from grandma's
unsold house—high on meth or heroin
or maybe not high at all but fighting
her hunger—while I pick through this dead
girl's jewelry just as starved for something
to hold onto as those feckless gulls pecking

the sand a few feet away. The sun is shining
brighter than the gold-plated necklace
I fasten around my neck and swear to wear
forever, and even though scientists are finding
nicotine in the water and oxy in the mussels,
my cousin's kids are down there at the edge
of the beach screaming their heads off
with the pure joy of plunging below the surface.
It's hard not to feel good watching the waves.
But my aunt needs me to believe in the glass
and the blood, and her daughter's body
a thing unidentifiable, a thing none of us
had really seen in years. She needs me to understand
that her pain is water as far as the eye can see.

Spring Letter from the South

Mother, it's like summer here. I miss
        the way the mountains get cold at night,
draw their shoulders up. In the evenings

        we walk through the old neighborhoods,
                past the frayed houses where magnolias
collapse their heavy bosoms against

        each roof's pitched elbows. Everything
the baby does—proclaiming song-words
           to the birds, commanding trees

               to hold still or spill their guts—
is magic I haven't given up on yet.
        That pollen-rot smell is starting again:

one year later and it's like a year
        hasn't passed. When she sleeps pressed against
           me, we still feel so young—all of us.

Even the cemetery is beautiful
        this time of year. Do you remember
when you were here? It's like that.

Anemoia

Not yet old enough to read, and already
      my daughter's learned nostalgia by example,
what to feel at a loon's call or when passing
      a blue door, how the sky just before nightfall
turns like a vulnerable animal showing
      its belly. She misses the dog who died
before she was born, the town we barely
      lived in. When she tries to give language
to everything she thinks as *past*—the Indians
      and ice caps and the neighbor girl now
ten states away who used to thread flowers
      through her baby-fine hair—her words
become the ropes that lower each to its grave.
      I want to cut loose from her each wistful sigh
I hear escape her lips, lips that have never
      spoken secrets like scars on the air or kissed
another's mouth to bruising. But if she doesn't
      learn nostalgia now, how will I ever teach her
regret? I have to get her ready for the future.

Still Life with Caviar and Crayons

The Russian Vodka Room isn't what it
used to be, not like when you lived here.
A bit shabbier, more well-lit so the wear
on the vinyl seats shows, no one at the piano,
a thin string of Christmas lights marking off
the hallway to the bathroom. And yet, here's Olga—
could it really be the same?—taking a break
from her romance novel to wave you in
as her voice writes some indecipherable Cyrillic
into the air over her shoulder. She brings out caviar,
blinis, crème fraîche and dumplings, then four icy
vials of terrible vodka: garlic pepper and dill,
apricot pear, horseradish, and finally
strawberry. This could almost be you again,
but for your daughter uptown, running circles
in the hotel room, crayons scattered across
the bedspread where she's napped all week
between trips to the museum, the park, the kosher
brunch you can't get anywhere else. There's something
so wretched about trying to revisit the past,
as if it's out there in the ether hanging on
and waiting for you: the lovers you'd forgive
if you could, the pleasure you'd remind yourself
to feel, the luck you'd know enough to be grateful for.
That better version of yourself you've become
with time, but beautiful still, nothing
weighting you to this tired November ground.
But the world is older, too, isn't it? No one's
waiting out there for you to find that bookmark
you planted in the past. Shabbier,
yes, more well-lit. Everything suddenly clear
as the vodka in Olga's outstretched hand.

Names of Rivers

Love, the dogwoods are fish shaking loose
       their pale scales.

I like it when you're not here
       so I can tell you what you're missing:

a skein of black dirt stretched
       like lace across the kitchen floor

and through the windows
       two birds tussling in a sea of felled petals.

The river was once a place for me
       to drown myself, tying to my ankles

the weight of what I'd lost, then jumping in:
       Tensaw, Paint Rock, Coosa, Sipsey,

Cahaba, Mobile, Chattahoochee, Pea.
       Nothing could have stopped me

from my own agreement with regret.
       Now the river is for showing me

the uselessness of sharp edges,
       how each thing that curves away

is not a body resisting but a pleasure
       waiting to be reciprocated.

When you come home, there's nothing
       that won't be waiting for you.

In the Yard I Lie on My Back and Dream of Turtles

Or would if I were asleep, and not awake
while this child runs circles around the star

of my limbs pinned to the ground. She brings me
the yellowest leaf, the thinnest stick,

each perfectly round pebble she finds
hidden in the grass beneath my body's

sharpest points. She piles them on the belly
that was her first home, this belly

that sleeps now like a sea calmed.
She is making something new

of me, something to someday burn
only in the quiet ditch of her memory,

a body subsumed by earth, carrying
the new world on a shell made of bone.

At the Halloween Party

There are not enough drinks
to keep me from losing
my mind. Between the swamp
of princess costumes, I retrieve
a memory of my mother
dressed as a gypsy—
flounced skirt, silk handkerchief,
her long fingers playing
over the body of a plastic
recorder as she danced
across the room, dazzling
my brother and me with her beauty,
her knowledge of everything
at the age I am now.
My body can't make
another child. We're both
done trying. Tonight on the street
I recognized my old
suede coat, the red one I took
to the thrift store last week.
College coat, party coat,
contraception-tucked-in-the-pocket
coat. Coat of my hair
long and ungrayed and falling
to the knee-length hem.
Tonight it worked its magic
again, transforming a girl
with stethoscope and horns
into a doctor devilish and
slick as any I've met. Seeing
her in it makes me, too,
a kind of fiction: my body
a broken promise, a cup
of coldening cider,

a pumpkin carved to look
like a cloud of bats on
furious, dying fire.

Abatement

Joel's here to check the termite stations
buried in our yard like time capsules,

to spray the sills with poison fine as French
perfume wafting from a lady's wrist

and sprinkle grains of acid over anthills
risen in red clay cupcakes from the edges

of the drive. Joel doesn't wear gloves, a mask—
just dons a Sunday school smile before he asks

if I'd like the lawn where my daughter lolls
blanket-sprayed for mosquitos. And when

he and I bring this world to its sure end, what
will be the best we can hope for then? An afternoon

not unlike this one: palmetto bugs testing the air
with their antennae, waiting to see who'll come next.

Collaborators

Walking at night, I read the house numbers
on those porches lit like vacant stairwells

hung along the mill's lip, flights of metal
steps any type of weather might fall through,

and this gentle litany tolls the schedule
of departing ferries that take us from

island to city and back again—1210,
1245—ferries where the whales bloom

a black and white skirt in our wake, ferries
we drive our big cars onto because now

we can go anywhere, ferries that took
the people from the clear shore of their lives

to the internment camps on the mainland
because nothing could be more dangerous

than living among each other where voices
unnetted and rising in complaint

are a flock of birds that can make no better
song than that one which we sing together.

Essentials

At the U-pick, I reach up
under the rustling green
hems, past the barbed
limbs, to the fruit, nipple-dark
and quickening to sugar
at my touch. Is it any wonder
I think of the first time
my hands strayed
beneath your shirt,
the dumb notes
that played on my palms
crushing the held
breath from me?
But that was years ago,
when we had reasons
for keeping secrets.
These days we watch
the locals make wine,
visit other people's castles
opened to the public
where we take in
the garden and the pool
where the poet drowned
now filled in with stones
raked into shapes meant
to calm the mind.
Now, when we walk
the beach, anything we find
too perfect is made
of plastic. I have seen
the oceans. I don't need
to lose anything else.

After the Farmers Market, I Make a Salade Niçoise

The fingerlings slip, faded yellow pearls,
from my palms. Purple pole beans and flax wax—

I slice them down their slender lengths, blanched
now into brightness. Then a sack of dun

olives, oil-shined and speckled with scarce thyme,
precious as a clutch of glossed tanager eggs.

Just one small packet of smoked black cod—rich,
musky—gifted me from the frozen gut

of an Alaskan fishing boat. At last,
I crack delicate shells, pull something poached

and trembling from the water's curled lip.
The loose-limbed teens who sold me my vegetables—

not so much younger than myself, and yet
young enough I might once have made them—

could only have spent last night crushing
zucchini blossoms, fucking under fired

stars, their bodies and the last fleshy hours
of another day ripening beyond

all recognition, the reaped and the wasted,
in this shallow bowl where we lay it all.

Teaching Day Aubade

This anxious spring, two
of my students become lovers,
and on Tuesday evenings
I walk home after class
under the unimaginably
tender buds of the still-spare
limbs that seam this star-flecked
air. Across town, the new pair
climb the staircase to his rooms,
their hands another set
of constellated branches
hopelessly entwined.
Light from the hallway
stretches its thin neck
across the bed, her bare
feet. He puts on some music.
And when she goes
for a glass of water and finds
his plate in the sink—a gleaming,
pockmarked moon—she lifts
one damp crumb on her fingertip
and presses it, like an old-fashioned
stamp, to her tongue. The poems
we read in class today run
through them now like fish to sea—
their urgency, their flash.

After My Shower, a Bee at the Window

She crawls against the pane, belly-dragging
her reflection below wings poised for flight.

My own mirror fogged with steam, I lean in
for a look: it likes to tell me I'm young,

but without the wink and nod of glass, I
know my body is close to learning some

new thing about itself. This was to be
my poem of transformation, for which I

find I can't now see beyond my toes. She
asks, *Where do you go when you're not here?*

As if my vision will uncloud and I'll know
the name my body's longing to become.

I cup her in my hand where she buzzes
like a chainsaw before I lift the sash.

Digging Out the Splinter

It is not a metaphor. We huddled
together by the bedside lamp, passing

the needle back and forth, neither of us
able to work it out. Later, she left

to wash the dishes, and I kept at it
until I found what we had sought. I stayed

in the bedroom, testing the point against
my palm, watching the sky out the window

grow deep. I could hear her in the kitchen,
and when the noises stopped, I knew she, too,

had found some question of her own to chase.
I read a poem, which after all is not

the same as life. And I was glad, I saw—
despite all our sorrows—to be married.

Wife

Butterfly wing, shark's tooth, quill.

What if I don't want to be human anymore,
every *thing* placed behind its plate of glass?

And the porcupine outside my window—

when I tiptoe through the frosted grass
to where she chews the red bud from the shale—

what is it I long to take from her? Shall I pull

a needle from the sweet nettle of her tail
and thread it tender through my lobe?

If only I could hold myself so close to the ground,

my body over the stones making a robe
of seamless understanding, a comfort not

unlike forgiveness. Tell me if this is the promise

you've been waiting to untie like a knot.
The Sufis say mercy is the act of disguising

another's faults. Even the universe must

have its own humility—the sky gently prizing
loose each dead star, the minor keys winking out

like my lids when you kiss them goodnight.

Told You So

When my daughter spills her orange juice, I wipe it off the linoleum

with the old plaid boxers of the man I thought I'd marry.
      Elastic ripped out, seams unraveling—I've had lives
already. At night they crawl across

my skin before I can turn on the light.
      We spend all these years wanting, and then one day—sudden
as a lamp set to a timer—we have.

There were the nights I drank just so I could feel a little
      more of my own unhappiness. Now, with my feet pressed
into this rug, I'll never be that drunk again.

Before I went to the clinic to get pregnant, I cried onto the shoulder
      of an old flame, worried that whoever I loved next would never
know my body when it was beautiful.

How could I have been wrong about so many things?

We drive home from the lake, sand in our shoes,

the dart of fish faint at our ankles, each
shuttered BBQ shack a kudzu flash

in my side mirror. Pleasure has become
the itch of a mosquito bite between

my shoulders, and your rough thumb on my thigh
a tickle gentle as turtles bobbing

in Sea-Doo oil slick and cellophane scraps.
How many years did I suffer the loves

that gave too much freedom and not enough
tenderness? Let me be like the man we

saw outside of Notasulga, hands cuffed
behind his back, cigarette in his mouth,

and you be the sheriff, leaning in close,
cupping the sweet flame to my waiting face.

Still Life with Beauty Berries and Two Theories of Time

It is as though time has been compressed and—as if looking through a telescope—things seem closer than they really are. The opposite is called backward or reverse telescoping, also known as time expansion.
—Claudia Hammond, *Time Warped: Unlocking the Mysteries of Time Perception*

In the first, I am
changing her diapers,
swabbing her new flesh
with tentative fingers,
then pressing her
face to my breast as if
to smother her in
the dark perfume
of my aging sweat.
Those days and nights
run together like a stream
flooded, busted into
the new pasture,
grass twisting under
the pressure's flow.
Now she points
to her chest and commands,
Tickle heart, Mama.
She wants me to kiss her
diaper rash, give her
a doctor's "poke"
beside her tiny starburst
nipple, and calls herself
baby, little baby
as an excuse to put
her mouth on me again.
But she's a girl with the dog's
ear between her teeth, throwing

stones over the fence
and bringing me handfuls
of beauty berries, astringent
delicacies for the birds, asking
me to part my lips. *Poison,*
I say, *poison,* my breath sweet
with the burnt sugar smell
of everything that's past.

Notes

Still Life with Nursing Bra" is indebted to Elizabeth Bradfield for a guest workshop she taught at Auburn University on close attention to objects.

All poems entitled "Still Life with . . ." are the result of a collaboration with visual artist Erica Harney.

"Migration Instinct" is for Becky Brunson.

"Self-Care at the Playground" was written in the months following the killing of Philando Castile and is an attempt to reckon with the reflexive passivity of many white Americans in the face of the ongoing murder of black men, women, and children in our country. In this regard, the poem is a failure. More information on the value of the public practice of failure can be found in my introduction to *Poetry Northwest*'s series "On Failure" (www.poetrynw.org/on-failure-introduction/).

The epigraph for "Outside the Refugium" is from *Home Ground: A Guide to the American Landscape* edited by Barry Lopez and Debra Gwartney (Trinity University Press, 2013).

"The Great Lakes" is written in memory of my cousin Julie Ann Shaffer, who left behind three boys who were the joy of her life.

The title "Anemoia" comes from *The Dictionary of Obscure Sorrows,* which is an online compendium of invented words written by John Koenig. "Anemoia" is a noun, meaning "nostalgia for a time you've never known." I am indebted to Raye Hendrix for suggesting the title for this poem.

"Collaborators" was written in response to the signing on January 27, 2017, of Executive Order 13769, titled "Protecting the Nation from Foreign Terrorist Entry into the United States" and known informally as "the Muslim travel ban." Seventy-five years earlier, on March 30, 1942, the internment of Japanese Americans under Executive Order 9066 began with 227 residents of Bainbridge Island, Washington, who were taken from their homes and incarcerated in what would become the Manzanar War Relocation Center in California (www.historylink.org/File/8277).

The epigraph for "Still Life with Beauty Berries and Two Theories of Time" is from *Time Warped: Unlocking the Mysteries of Time Perception* by Claudia Hammond (Harper Perennial, 2013).

Acknowledgments

Grateful acknowledgment is made to the editors of the following publications, in which these works or earlier versions of them previously appeared:

32 Poems: "Springtime Makes Us Want";

About Place: "Names of Rivers";

Alaska Quarterly Review: "At Golden Gate Park with You," "Landscape Without";

The Believer: "Shooting Clay Pigeons After the Wedding";

Birmingham Poetry Review: "First Trimester";

Blackbird: "At the Arlee Pow-Wow with My Unborn Child," "Getting the Baby to Sleep";

Cheat River Review: "Georgia";

Cherry Tree: "Still Life with Beauty Berries and Two Theories of Time," "Still Life with Ocean and Nearly Dead Dog";

Codex: "Migration Instinct," "Told You So";

Construction: "Donetsk";

Crab Creek Review: "Ars Poetica Composed in Exile," "Love Note";

Ecotone: "The House on Fish Hatchery Road," "Outside the Refugium";

Fogged Clarity: "Becoming," "My Brother Says My Milk Smells Different";

Gigantic Sequins: "On Needing to See a River";

Gulf Coast: "We drive home from the lake, sand in our shoes,";

Hunger Mountain: "At the Small Town Drag Show";

Kenyon Review: "Collaborators";

The Literary Review: "In the Yard I Lie on My Back and Dream of Turtles," "Still Life with Nursing Bra";

The Los Angeles Review: "After My Shower, a Bee at the Window," "Glassblower's Glossary of Flaws and Defects," "Yardwork";

Narrative: "Anemoia," "Essentials," "Self-Care at the Playground," "Picking Huckleberries as the World Ends," "Wife";

NELLE: "Abatement";

New England Review: "Landscape with Sage and the Names of My Children";

Orion: "Landscape with Child," "Native Species";

The Pinch: "Outside the New Body";

Poetry Northwest: "The elk my father shot," "I buy my white daughter a black doll";

Raleigh Review: "Spring Letter from the South";

A River and Sound Review: "At the Museum of Trades and Traditions";

The Rumpus: "Still Life with Caviar and Crayons," "Teaching Day Aubade";

Southern Indiana Review: "After the Farmers Market, I Make a Salade Niçoise," "At the Halloween Party," "Laying On of Hands," "On the Haunted Hayride with Audrey";

Tin House: "The Great Lakes";

TriQuarterly: "Still Life with Small Objects of Perfect Choking Size."

"We drive home from the lake, sand in our shoes," was reprinted in *The Best American Poetry 2016* (Scribner, 2016) and in *The Mind Has Cliffs of Fall: Poetry at the Extremes* (W. W. Norton & Company, Inc., 2019.

"Still Life with Small Objects of Perfect Choking Size" was reprinted in *Still Life with Poem: 100 Natures Mortes in Verse* (Literary House Press, 2016).

"Migration Instinct" was reprinted in *The Pushcart Prize XL: Best of the Small Presses 2016 Edition* (Pushcart Press, 2015).

"Georgia" was reprinted in *Stone, River, Sky: An Anthology of Georgia Poems* (Negative Capability Press, 2015).

Thanks to Lindsay Doukopoulos and Cate Lycurgus, who read early versions of many of these poems. I still cherish your handwritten notes. Thanks to Dorianne Laux, who provided generous feedback on the first version of this manuscript as part of my reward for winning the Field Office's 2015 Postcard Prize. Special thanks to Erika Meitner, whose comments on this manuscript were crucial, and to Megan Snyder-Camp, who sacrificed part of a writing residency to an invaluable discussion of these poems. A giant hug to my Poetry Gals—Gabrielle Bates, Rachel Edelman, and Abi Pollokoff—who read these poems individually and then as a whole. I will always feel blessed (as they say in Alabama) for the space you made for me in your writing community. Special thanks, too, to Erin Malone, who was of indispensable assistance in ordering this collection, and who, along with her husband, Shawn Wong, offered the use of their quiet cottage on the coast where I was able to put this book through its paces. I am grateful to the following institutions, which provided vital fellowships, residencies, and financial support during the crafting of this manuscript: the Alabama State Council on the Arts, Auburn University, the Bread Loaf Writers' Conference, Gettysburg College, the Jentel Artist Residency Foundation, the Lucas Artist Residency Program at Montalvo Center for the Arts, and PLAYA. Heartfelt thanks to Chantel Acevedo and Ken Autrey, who made Alabama a place where my poems could grow for a time. And thanks, too, to the good folks at Hugo House and *Poetry Northwest,* who have made me feel so welcome in my new teaching and editing homes in Seattle. To my BOA family: your steadfast support and enthusiasm have grounded my writing for nearly a decade—I know how lucky I am. And thanks, finally, to my wife, Sarah, and our daughter, Nela, who have given me a life full of more love than any I could ever have imagined.

About the Author

Keetje Kuipers has been a Stegner Fellow and the Margery Davis Boyden Wilderness Writing Resident. A recipient of the Pushcart Prize, her poems, essays, and short stories have appeared in such publications as *American Poetry Review, Orion, Tin House,* and *The Best American Poetry.* She is also the author of two previous poetry collections, *Beautiful in the Mouth* and *The Keys to the Jail.* Senior editor at *Poetry Northwest* and faculty at Seattle's Hugo House, Kuipers lives with her wife and daughter on an island in the Salish Sea, where she is at work on a novel and a memoir.

BOA Editions, Ltd., American Poets Continuum Series

Colophon

BOA Editions, Ltd., a not-for-profit publisher of poetry and other literary works, fosters readership and appreciation of contemporary literature. By identifying, cultivating, and publishing both new and established poets and selecting authors of unique literary talent, BOA brings high-quality literature to the public. Support for this effort comes from the sale of its publications, grant funding, and private donations.

✳

The publication of this book is made possible, in part,
by the support of the following individuals:

Anonymous
Nickole Brown & Jessica Jacobs
Rick Bursky
Charles E. Coté
Dr. Jenny Graber
James Long Hale
Joe McElveney
Boo Poulin
Deborah Ronnen
Steven O. Russell & Phyllis Rifkin-Russell
David W. Ryon
William Waddell & Linda Rubel
Michael Waters & Mihaela Moscaliuc